MW00769972

BUILDING YOUR BAND OF BROTHERS

Just a Few of Stephen Mansfield's Books

Mansfield's Book of Manly Men

The Character and Greatness of Winston Churchill:
Hero in a Time of Crisis

Then Darkness Fled:
The Liberating Wisdom of Booker T. Washington

Forgotten Founding Father:
The Heroic Legacy of George Whitefield

The Search for God and Guinness

Lincoln's Battle with God

BUILDING YOUR BAND OF BROTHERS

STEPHEN MANSFIELD

BLACKWATCH
DIGITAL

Author photograph: Isaac Darnall

Published in Nashville, Tennessee by Blackwatch Digital.

(print) ISBN: 978-0-9977647-9-6
(ebook) ISBN: 978-0-9977647-6-5

"We few,

We happy few,

We band of brothers."

—William Shakespeare, Henry V

"The mass of men lead lives of quiet desperation, and go to the grave with the song still in them."

—*Henry David Thoreau*

"Real friendships among men are so rare that when they occur they are famous."

—*Clarence Day*

"The making of friends, who are real friends, is the best token we have of a man's success in life."

—*Edward Everett Hale*

"No man is the whole of himself; his friends are the rest of him."

—*Harry Emerson Fosdick*

TABLE OF CONTENTS

GENTLEMEN, WE BEGIN . . .

I WANT YOU TO IMAGINE SOMETHING WITH ME. WHATEVER YOUR HIS-
tory, whatever your race or your native country, I want you to roll
the story of your people back a few hundred years in your mind.
Think about the men at that time. Remind yourself of how they
lived and of what sealed them to each other.

These men—your ancestors—probably lived their whole
lives in vital connection to other men. It determined nearly
everything about them. In fact, it determined the meaning of
manhood itself. What they knew and what they lived is part of
what we need to recover today.

Keep imagining the lives of our ancestors with me. A few
centuries ago families were often large, unless disease or war
reduced their size. A man was likely to have brothers. He grew
up with these companions, explored the world with them, and
learned with them all that their parents had to teach. Often a

man and his brothers lived near each other all their days, standing together against the onslaughts of the world and building together the things that made life worth living.

These brothers were also part of a larger band of men: the men of the village, town, or tribe. Survival was impossible without them. The men of this wider male community depended on each other for defense. They needed each other for the hunt. They relied on each other for help with their farms, for trade, and for the skills they did not possess themselves. They worked together, fought together, celebrated together, and worshipped together. During restful moments, they traded jokes, talked about the ways of the world, and entrusted each other with their dreams. They were tightly knit, an essential part of each other's lives.

These were the commitments that bound men together centuries ago. They lived open, accountable, dutiful lives. They were connected. They had roles to play, jobs to do. They were devoted to a people—their people.

Introverts had to get over themselves. Loners were suspect. A man without a people to call his own was often viewed as a threat. If he was rootless and untethered, he might also be lawless and unprincipled. This was how people thought several hundred years ago.

Sometimes we forget these truths from our history and believe myths instead. Americans, for example, have a soft place in their hearts for the image of the solitary man on horseback who rode out into the western frontier. It's true that there were men who ventured into the wilderness on their own like this and a few even built colorful reputations, but communities built the nation. Two hundred years ago, most men would have thought that a guy who went into the wild alone was a fool.

Life as part of a company of men was the way of our ancestors, but it is far from the way of men today. The majority of men today have no meaningful connection to other men. They have no band of brothers. They do not belong to a people. They do not belong—anywhere. Instead, most men today live lonely, rootless, untethered lives.

It is killing them. Surveys confirm it. Medical studies confirm it. The male suicide rate confirms it.[1]

Fortunately, the average man today can still vaguely remember what it was like when he had friends. When he was a boy, his friends were everything. He came home from that first day of school and his mother asked him if he had made any new friends. The answer was important. In the days after, he rushed through his chores and homework to be with his buddies. They were his world, or at least the companions who explored the world with him.

3

This didn't change much during his teen years. Sports, music, cars, goofing off, and the unending pursuit of girls sealed him to other guys. They were his tribe. They were his band of boisterous brothers.

This likely continued all through high school. Friendships were easier to find in those days. They were right at hand. Buddies lived in the same neighborhood or attended the same school or played in the same band or found each other at the same part-time jobs and during the raucous hours of fun that never seemed to end back then—back when friends were easier to find. If he went to college, this all continued for years more.

Then, it started to happen. School came to an end. Our man went to work. He got married. He had children. Or maybe he stayed single. It doesn't matter. The same forces took control. There were obligations. There were a couple of moves. His company required it. Maybe the military required it, or the search for hard-to-find jobs.

Whatever the cause, he got separated from his buddies. He got busy. A friend stopped being someone to hang out with every spare moment and became someone to call on the phone a few times a year. This kind of degraded friendship so marks our generation that psychologists have a name for it. They call them "rust" friends. It means guys who used to be close but who now only check in with each other a few times a year. Rust has grown on the friendship. It isn't crucial anymore. It's just there. It's more a memory than a present reality.

This is all most men have today—a few rusty friendships. It isn't the way it was meant to be. This is why the average guy today longs for the meaningful connections he once had to other men. Like most males in the Western world, he's convinced he has lost those friendships forever and will never get them back again.

I have lived this way.

I'm guessing you have too.

If our average guy has indeed lost meaningful connection to other men, the tragedy is that he has also lost the good they once brought to his life. He remembers it well. He remembers that they made him better.

His buddies saw him get tongue-tied and pitiful around girls and they said something. They may have been harsh and embarrassing, but they pointed out what needed to be fixed. They did the same when it came to his driving or his guitar playing or his silly clothes or his ridiculous way of holding a bat. They were his pack. The pack fixed things. The pack brought him into line.

He was better in his pack, even if its corrections sometimes drew blood. He worked harder at everything he did because of the pack. He did more push-ups. He didn't hog the ball. He was

5

smoother with girls. He also studied harder. He didn't want to be the class idiot. The pack would notice. The pack would say something. So, he learned. He grew. He got better.

The average man today has none of this in his life. He has no men around him. He has no pack. No one is pushing him to be better. No one nips at him when he's out of line. Who drives him to his best? Where are the men who see him for what he is and what he can be and won't shut up until he gets on with the improving? There's no one near. Only distant, rusty friendships survive.

This need for a pack, for a band of brothers, becomes all the more urgent when our guy glimpses the meaning of true manhood. This is when he begins realizing what he was meant to be. He begins understanding that he's allowed himself to be defined by his lusts, his loneliness, and his wounds. He starts to grieve this. He starts to grieve his distance from God and from the man he is called to be. He also grieves what masculinity has become in his generation. He wants to be part of a change.

As he comes home to a new vision of manhood, it dawns on him that he cannot achieve it alone. He needs men around him to help him. He needs the eyes of others on him. He needs a team, a pack, a band of brothers—all committed to the noble project of achieving valiant manhood. He finally accepts the truth that nearly always launches men to new heights: we are better together.

Here's how I say it and I often say it aloud just to rivet this truth to my soul: "I need other men in my life to be the man I am called to be."

You should say this yourself: "I need other men in my life to be the best man I can be."

Now, let's go further. Here is the truth you need to know: the band of brothers you need won't form by itself. The men you need in your life in order for you to become a great man won't assemble on their own. Few of us live the lives our ancestors did. Most of us don't have a natural community of men around us. This means we have to be intentional about this business of building a band of brothers. It means that you are going to have to go after it and make it happen.

Living your life in a band of brothers is what this book is about. This is a hard-hitting, practical, distinctly masculine guide to the art of building a band of brothers. You will feel an urgency in these pages. It comes from the certainty that most men are in danger as long as they live their lives apart from a thriving community of men. In fact, you may very well be in danger now as you read these words. You wouldn't be alone. This explains some of the fire, even the ferocity, that fills every page you are about to read.

You and the men of this generation must reclaim the art of building a band of brothers. Manhood in our time depends upon it. Manhood in your life depends upon it. Generations to come may depend upon it too.

Gentlemen, let's get to it.

Time to Build

1. Do you know of a time in your family's history when men were close and helped each other in life? If so, is it the same today? What changed?

2. Do you see yourself in Stephen's description of today's isolated man? If so, was it always that way? What changed to make your life what it is today? If not, how are you able to avoid the isolation plaguing most men today?

3. Describe how a "pack" or group of invested friends has made you better at times in your life. Do you still have such friends? If not, why not?

4. Stephen insists that the band of brothers you need won't form by itself. You'll have to create it. Why do you suppose this is true? What changes will you have to make to start creating a band of brothers? What are you excited about as you begin? What scares you a bit?

THE FOOL WHO
WALKED ALONE

GENTLEMEN, I CAN SPEAK OF THE THINGS I HAVE DESCRIBED IN THE
previous chapter because I have lived them. Let me tell you a bit
about this.

I grew up the son of a United States Army officer. My
father's career meant that my family moved constantly. I played
three sports a year and had a devoted band of crazy friends at
each of my father's posts. It was a good life—as long as it lasted.
Each spring, though, it would all come to an end. My family
would move and all my friends would be lost. I seldom ever saw
any of them again.

The conventional wisdom is that military brats don't put
down roots, they put out vines. It's true. When you know you're
going to be uprooted constantly, you don't go deep. You don't
plant. You live lightly so that when the inevitable move comes it
won't be so painful. I did this.

It didn't help that I was also an introvert. I found time alone more interesting than time with people. Sure, I had my buddies, but I didn't let them into my heart as much as I might have because I knew the agonizing move was always just ahead and because people tended to crowd into that quiet place in my skull where I spent most of my time.

I eventually went to a university that drew students from all over the world. It was a thrilling experience but it also meant that everyone I knew was from someplace else. Though I spent five wonderful years at that school, after graduation everyone I knew dispersed to the four corners of the earth. Once again, I seldom saw any of them again.

I did manage to keep in contact with a few close buddies from my college years. Their friendships are dear to me to this day, but we have never lived within five hundred miles of each other and so nearly everything we know about each other's lives we've learned over the phone. I admit it. Rust has set in.

The usual things happened. A job. A marriage. Then children. I was grateful for it all but I did not know at the time what I know now: I had become disconnected from the band of men I needed. My duties and responsibilities became barriers to the very relationships with men that would have made me better at my duties and responsibilities—that would have made me a better man.

The Fool Who Walked Alone

I had work friends. I had racquetball friends. I had some church friends. I did not have a band of brothers. I did not have men who knew my life and could see what I could not see about myself. I did not have men who were not afraid of me, who would say whatever needed to be said to make me better and with whom life was a rowdy joy.

In other words, I was like most men today. I was alone. I was declining. The fires of manhood were growing dim in my soul.

What saved me was a crisis. I came to a terrible time in my life and it forced me to face the fact that I was awash in a sea of casual relationships. I had employees and acquaintances, but I had no one who was willing to join me at the front lines of my life and help me be a good and noble man. I certainly had no one to say the tough things I needed to hear, to inspire me, to laugh with me, and to celebrate the victories when they came.

Fortunately, some tough, wise, experienced men stepped in just when I was about to give up hope. These men knew how to battle for a man's soul. They went to war for me. I want you to know that these dudes slammed into me harder than anyone ever had. I was just successful enough in those days to be proud, defensive, and blind to all that was wrong with me. These men spared me nothing. They didn't stop to notice how awesome I was—or how awesome I thought I was! They didn't take time for compliments and niceties. They just went to work chiseling, confronting, correcting, and, when necessary, reducing me to a weepy shell of my former self.

Thanks to their investment and the grace of God, I got through that horrible season. Things eventually got better in my life. Yet my newfound sense of the foolish way I had lived my life before the crisis stuck with me. In truth, it haunted me. I could see this same haunting in the eyes of men I passed on the street. In fact, my whole generation of men seemed a reflection of the deformed, lonely mess I had once been.

I began to see it clearly. What we have lost in our generation—in addition to a transforming connection to God—is the power of being part of a band of brothers. What we have lost is what our ancestors knew—that we are better together, that a man who is self-defined is defined by a fool and that no man achieves his best alone.

We will have to reclaim what these ancestors knew. We will have to restore a life of noble manhood pursued as part of a band of brothers. And we will have to be intentional about it. Our whole age works against men bonding meaningfully, joyfully, with other men to live out noble manhood.

It won't be easy. We will have to declare war on ourselves and on the deformed values of our times to make it happen, but there will be nothing so glorious as rebuilding what has been lost. There will be nothing so glorious as life lived among a band of brothers.

Time to Build

1. Stephen listed several reasons why he had trouble building long-lasting relationships when he was younger. First, he was an introvert. Second, since his family was military and moved a lot, he became better at putting out shallow vines rather than deep relational roots. Can you relate to either of these? How so? Is there another factor that kept you from building long-lasting male friendships when you were younger? How has this affected your adult relationships with men?

2. Who in your life, outside of your family, can you count on to join you at the front lines in your struggle to be a good and noble man? If you cannot name someone, why is that? Are all your relationships casual and somewhat shallow? What has kept you from taking any of those relationships to a deeper level? If you were able to name someone, describe how that relationship became deep and meaningful to you.

3. Stephen wrote: "We will have to declare war on ourselves and on the deformed values of our time" in order to truly build our own band of brothers. What are these "deformed values"? How have you allowed yourself to buy into them? What might it look like to "declare war" on yourself and our generation's

15

deformed values? What obstacles are you likely to face in this "war"?

THE MEANING OF "BAND OF BROTHERS"

IN THE DAYS OF THE ROMAN EMPIRE, THERE WERE TWO CHRISTIAN brothers who lived in the region that today is France. Their names were Crispin and Crispinian. They were shoemakers whose deep commitment to the example of Jesus moved them to give generously to the poor. Their fierce faith was the reason Roman authorities decided to execute them. The exact date this occurred is lost to us, but the Christian church honors these two martyrs each year on October 25, a date that has come to be known as St. Crispin's Day.

More than a thousand years after these two brothers were killed, England and France were at war. Before one of the great battles of that war, a battle at a place called Agincourt, King Henry V of England gave a rousing speech to his troops. This occurred on St. Crispin's Day—Friday, October 25, 1415.

We don't know exactly what the king said but witnesses reported that it was one of the most moving speeches they had ever heard. A century later, William Shakespeare imagined that moment and made it part of his stirring *Henry V*. Shakespeare's version of Henry's words, one of the great speeches in all of English literature, is known to history as the St. Crispin's Day Speech. In it are these lines:

We few,

We happy few,

We band of brothers,

For he today that sheds his blood with me,

Shall be my brother.

It was William Shakespeare, then, who gave us the words "band of brothers." For centuries, warriors had referred to their "brothers at arms" or "brothers in battle," but Shakespeare's phrase captured the bond among men so succinctly and poetically that it has lived vibrantly through the generations.

Admiral Horatio Nelson used the phrase in 1798 to inspire his men prior to the Battle of the Nile. Some unit commanders quoted the entire St. Crispin's Day speech to their troops before the Allied landing at Normandy on D-Day in 1944. In the more recent wars in Afghanistan and Iraq, a new generation of commanders have often done the same.

In fact, Shakespeare's phrase so perfectly captured this powerful masculine ideal that it was used in the song intended as the first US national anthem. That song was called "Hail, Columbia" and was written by Joseph Hopkinson. In it were the following words:

> Firm, united, let us be,
> Rallying round our Liberty;
> As a band of brothers joined,
> Peace and safety we shall find.

In recent decades, this magnificent phrase has become even more widely known. It was the title of a book and TV miniseries about the famed E Company, 506th Regiment, 101st Airborne, and its campaigns during World War II. The sacrifices and heroism of E Company only added luster to the words "band of brothers" and helped make the phrase more popular than William Shakespeare could ever have imagined.

For many men today, Shakespeare's words are deeply personal. For them, "band of brothers" evokes not only the bond among men in battle but the bond among men in every endeavor of life. It has come to mean those men whom a man cherishes, with whom he does life, and who are willing to invest with him in pursuit of righteous manhood. It describes those happy warriors who strive together to become the men they are destined to be.

Band of brothers. It is a phrase conceived in the martyrdom of Roman Christians. It was born of the pen of William Shakespeare, inspired as he was by a noble king and an epic battle. It has become a tool of leadership honed in battles through the centuries. Now, it is the language of our hopes that men might walk together in pursuit of the greatness for which they were made.

May it be so in your life. May you cease to walk alone, and instead be able to claim these words as your own:

We few,

We happy few,

We Band of Brothers.

Time to Build

1. Shakespeare wrote in Henry V, "For he today that sheds his blood with me, shall be my brother." Outside of an actual military or physical battle, what might "shedding one's blood" with another look like today? Who in your life would you be willing to "shed blood" with? Who in your life would do the same for you?

2. How would you differentiate between the phrases "brothers at arms" or "brothers in battle," and "band of brothers"? Though you may never have been a soldier in a military battle and so have never had a literal "brother at arms," you still need a band of brothers to stand with you in the battles of your life. Can you put this need for a band of brothers in your own words?

3. Stephen wrote that a man's band of brothers refers to men "whom a man cherishes, with whom he does life, and who are willing to invest with him in pursuit of righteous manhood." What do you think it means to "do life" with another man? What is appealing to you about having this type of friendship? What, if you're being completely honest with yourself, is not so appealing?

21

Building Your Band of Brothers

WHAT IS A BAND OF BROTHERS?

GENTLEMEN, LET US BE CLEAR FROM THE START. A BAND OF BROTHERS, in the sense that we use the words in this book, is not a meeting, a club, a therapy group, or a self-help society. It is the group of men we do life with. It is the team of brothers committed with us to the cause of great manhood. It is the band of men with whom we build a manly culture of inspiration and achievement.

Do not accept any substitutes.

Some men get involved in study groups thinking that if they study manhood with other guys then it will magically form in their lives. Together they read good books on masculinity and discuss them by the hour. Reading is good. Discussion is good. Still, they can't make you the man you are called to be.

Other men join "accountability groups." These are gatherings in which men tell each other what's going on in their lives. Then, there is discussion. Maybe prayer.

These groups don't tend to work either. Let me tell you why. If you are waiting for me to figure out what is wrong with me, hang on to that knowledge for two or three weeks until the next meeting, and then have the courage to drive across town and talk to you about it honestly over bacon and eggs—well, you'll be waiting a long time. And I'll be in trouble.

You see, we men, we lie! We "forget." We'll shade the truth to keep a friend or just to save our image. Most of us would rather die a slow death of some unchecked moral flaw than to ever open our lives to the scrutiny of other men. I'm not immune to this. Neither are you.

No, I need what you need. I need men walking closely enough with me to know who I am. I need men who love me but aren't afraid of me. I need men with whom I can experience the joy and wildness of being a man but who are also invested in me being all I can be—just as I am invested in them.

To be the finest man I can be, I need big brothers, little brothers, fathers, and just plain buddies. I need men who know what I can be and know what might keep me from it. I need men who can push me to my destiny.

Let me be even more specific. I need men who walk closely enough with me to notice the angry cell phone call I just had with my wife. They have to have the courage to mention it and ask what's going on. They help. They insist upon my best.

They are also near enough to know when I'm checking out the backside of the waitress. They point it out. They challenge me. They ask what's going on at home.

I want to walk through life with men who know that my particular problems aren't booze or women, but pride, foul language, and the twenty or thirty Oreos at a time that always seem like a good idea.

That's the deal. I need to do life with other men. And not, by the way, so they can keep me from messing up. That's part of it but not most of it. No, I need their example. I need their encouragement. I need their prayers. I need their hard-hitting challenges and their manly celebration of my victories. And, yes, I need for them to growl at me—even take a verbal swing at me—when I'm veering into trouble.

They need all of this from me too. Doing it together is what makes us a band of brothers.

I want to say it again. A band of brothers is not a meeting, a club, a therapy group, or a self-help society. It is the group of men we do life with.

I had a silly experience once that drove home one of the reasons I need men tightly around me. Perhaps you've had an experience like it.

I went to a party one night and had a grand old time. At some point during that evening, someone snapped a photo of me. Later, when they gave me a copy, I looked at it and asked who the guy in the photo was. My friend shot back, "It's you, fool!"

I looked again. Darn if he wasn't right. There I was scrunched down on a sofa. My head was jammed into my shirt. My shirt was stretched over my belly. My eyes were half closed, my mouth hung open stupidly, and my skin looked pasty and slack. In other words, I looked like Jabba the Hutt.

It was, I tell you, the ugliest photo ever taken of a human being. I genuinely did not recognize myself when I first saw it. The reason was simple: someone had caught me from a perspective I had never seen before. It was definitely me in the photo, but I had never seen that version of me.

You see, when I look in the mirror, my gut tightens, my neck extends, and I do my imitation of a bodybuilder pose. In the mirror, I'm *Stephen-the-Almost-Decent-Looking-Guy*. That's who I know, but I do not know *Stephen-as-Jabba-the-Hutt*.

I pondered that photo for a long time afterward. It occurred to me that if it is possible for me to be blind to how I could look on the outside, I might also be blind to who I really am on the inside. This meant I could be in danger. I could make a huge mess of my life. I might live my whole life as deceived about my inner realities as I apparently can be about my outer realities.

This small episode helped me realize I need the eyes of other men on me. I need a band of friends who together have a three-dimensional view of Stephen. I also need for them to use that perspective to help me get better, not to tear me down.

We are all like this. None of us can see ourselves, inside or out, with absolute clarity. None of us have enough insight into who we really are to coach ourselves. We need to be defined by God and others. We need to be guided by people who are near to us but different from us.

This entire episode convinced me of a truth that has never left me: the man who is self-defined—who lives only in the light of his own understanding of himself—is a fool. That's how I had been living. My guess is you've done this too. But we were fools. Some of us may still be. It's time to make a change.

Time to Build

1. Have you ever been part of a men's group? What was beneficial about the experience? Where did it come up short? What do you think keeps some men's groups from evolving into the "band of brothers" Stephen describes?

2. Stephen wrote, "Most of us would rather die a slow death of some unchecked moral flaw than to ever open our lives to the scrutiny of other men." Can you relate to this statement? What is it about "the scrutiny of other men" that deters most men from doing life with one another? How might we overcome this natural desire in men to keep their flaws hidden from each other?

3. Without seeing that candid picture taken of him at a party, Stephen would never have noticed how he could occasionally look to the rest of the world. Similarly, how can we get an accurate picture of what we look like on the inside? Do you have a man in your life who has ever dared to confront you about an issue in your life? Have you ever dared confront another man in the same way? If not, why not?

THE HEART OF
NOBLE MANHOOD

BEFORE WE GO FURTHER, WE SHOULD BRIEFLY DEFINE "noble manhood." I have done this already in my book *Mansfield's Book of Manly Men*, but you may not have read it yet and it is important that a clear picture forms in your mind when you read the word *manhood* in these pages.

I believe that the heart of great manhood, of noble manhood, is found in a very simple phrase: *Manly men tend their field.*[2] I take these words from the writings of a pretty manly guy named Paul the Apostle. In one of his letters to the Christians in ancient Corinth, he wrote, "We, however, will not boast beyond proper limits, but will confine our boasting to the sphere of service God himself has assigned to us, a sphere that includes you."[3]

In the middle of this verse is a word we cannot see because it is hidden behind the English translation. It is the word *metron,* the Greek word Paul used in his original letter. It means "a measured space." Even those of us who don't read Greek can see that the word *metron* is related to our English word *meter*, a unit of measure. I think the right English word for *metron* is "field." This makes the most sense of what Paul is trying to tell us.

Paul was saying three things to the Corinthians. First, God had assigned a field to him. Second, that field—like all fields—had boundaries. Third, that field contained everything for which God had given Paul responsibility. Paul was clear about where his lines of responsibility fell. He knew that the Corinthians were in his field of responsibility. The assumption is that he could have named other cities or people who were not his responsibility.

Now, I believe that what is true of Paul is also true of you and me. For every season of your life, God has given you a field to tend. That field is comprised of the people, things, and priorities God has assigned to you. Your job is to know your field, protect your field, and make sure that everything in your field flourishes according to the will of God.

This is what separates noble men from mere males. What summons true masculinity from the soul of a man is his decision to tend his God-assigned field with his God-given gifts for the glory of God and the good of others. That's when a man steps up. That is when he starts to draw on the resources of great manhood that lay dormant within him.

This doesn't mean that manhood is all duty. It doesn't mean that manhood is all drudgery and responsibility. It does mean that a man sets himself upon the path of noble manhood the moment he resolves to tend the field God has given him for each season of his life. That's when manly greatness begins.

I understand that what I am saying is radical. There are certainly other views. I know and admire leaders of men who believe we should emphasize the healing of the masculine soul or the recovering of manly wildness or freedom from our overly domesticated lives. There is truth in all of this.

My central belief, though, is that men are made to protect the territory assigned to them and to assure that everything within that territory fulfills its God-ordained purpose. This is what manhood is designed for. This is how a man fulfills his purpose. His decision to "own" his field moves both the best that is within him and the best that God has to offer into that partnership I call Great Manhood.

Everything noble and manly arises from this. The gifts of a man for standing guard. The power of a man's words to guide and encourage. The radiation of a man's presence and his capacity to stand down enemies with barely a word. His skill for scanning a scene and detecting threat or need for repair. The insight to envision a future and fashion a plan to achieve it. The ability of men to team up, assume tasks according to skill, and go to war. The fierce capacity of most men to love deep, love rowdy, and love with almost terrifying passion. These are just some of the gifts that begin to emerge in a man when he decides to tend his field to the glory of God.

There are other good things that begin to happen in a man's life when he starts using his gifts for God-ordained purposes. One of them is that he starts learning important things about himself. He discovers his true strengths. He recognizes his traits. He realizes his power.

He may have been aware of his gifts even before he began using them for God's purposes. It's likely, though, that he did not use them as they were intended. Instead, he used his gifts to dominate other men and to manipulate women and to serve his lesser drives. Once he decided to be what God has made him to be, he started to understand. Life is not about gaining the advantage. It is not about dominating. Life is about using your gifts for the glory of God, about "owning" the field you've been given, and about making everything in that field come into its destined state. Life is about taking the land according to the will and the ways of God.

A man who has decided to tend his field often makes other discoveries too. He may, for example, learn that something inside him isn't right. At some point in life, he has sustained damage. Since then, he hasn't lived with his inner systems fully engaged. He becomes aware of this because for the first time he has a noble goal, lives by a noble code, and sees in righteous examples around him what he is meant to be. This is how he learns he's sustained a debilitating injury.

He'll be all right, though. There's nothing to fear. He gets help. He gets healed. He fights back against the damage passed down through the generations and asks his band of brothers to stand with him as he does. He didn't know he'd been wounded so critically until he started taking responsibility for the health of those around him. That's when his God-given radar kicked in. That's when he detected something un-whole in himself and declared war on it so he could get on with being what he was meant to be.

Always his band of brothers—if he has one—is there to see him through. This is one of the benefits that comes to a man who has made the single decision to tend his field to the glory of God.

We get an even clearer picture of this core truth of great manhood—that manly men tend their field—when we recall one of our society's main images of the irresponsible man. This pathetic dude is glued to the recliner in front of his TV. His sweat pants are stained and his T-shirt is nasty. He could stand to lose about eighty pounds and to learn a thing or two about how a noble man makes himself presentable. This guy doesn't care, though. He's too busy yelling for someone to bring him another beer and sandwich before the second half of the game. He doesn't realize he's in need of work.

He also doesn't realize that his family is suffering from his neglect. His wife is somewhere else in the house nursing wounds her husband knows nothing about. She's bitter, resentful, gaining weight, and losing friends. Her soul gives every evidence of the lonely years she has lived with this foolish man.

His daughter is upstairs in her room getting ready for a night out. She's about to ride off with a guy who has destroyed the lives of many other young girls. Her father has no idea. He also has no idea that his daughter is carrying something in her purse that she's eager to keep from her parents. No one seems to have the courage to ask about it. Her father hasn't bothered to notice. Her mother has given up. Her brother spends all his time in his room in front of the computer with the door locked. He's too withdrawn and secretive—is it shame we see on his face?—to even notice the danger stalking his sister. Or, for that matter, stalking him.

In short, this man's family is in a free fall and it is all due to his neglect. Even his house is a symbol of his dysfunction. It was once beautiful and warm. Now it's crumbling, broken, and unloved. It feels alien, even to the family who lives there.

Everything in this man's life is suffering from the absence of noble manhood. He only takes up space. He does not tend his field. He is merely a tourist in his own life, a passerby who takes responsibility for nothing, who prays for nothing, who inter-venes for no noble purpose, and who is living so far from God's will that he reeks of the despair that has settled in his soul.

This is what it means for an uncaring man to neglect his field.

While we are thinking about cultural images of masculine neglect, we should give thought to another kind of man. This guy neglects the field assigned to him just as much as the idiot I described above. The problem is that he is so successful that his prosperity hides his neglect. His family lives in a large and beautiful house, his wife always looks stunning and drives an expensive car, and his kids go to the best schools and enjoy all the expensive toys our age has to offer.

Everything in this man's world looks perfect, from his hair to the vanity license plate on his Jaguar to the family photos on his desk. It's all just—well, perfect. Too perfect. The shiny exter-nals hide the reality that this man has given his heart to the pur-suit of success and bought his family off with money.

He's familiar with his wife's body but not her soul. He's proud of the fact that his daughter is the homecoming queen at her school but he has no idea what she does or who she is when she's not busy looking "fabulous!" And his son? Well, his son is the kid who's picking up the daughter of the first man we described. He's handsome and charming. He also uses girls the way his father uses him—as a tool for what he wants, as an adornment in his all-too-perfect world.

There's as much neglect going on in this second family as there is in the first. It's just that money shields the one and eludes the other.

Is this you?

We are called to more. We are called to a glorious purpose for every stage of our lives. The sixteen-year-old boy may have only half a bedroom, a rusty car, a job at the pizza place, a dating life, his schoolwork, and a few chores at home to be responsible for. Yet these things comprise his field. When he tends them well, to the glory of God and as wise and caring men advise him to do, good comes to him. He grows. He prospers. He moves eagerly to new fields with new responsibilities and new destined victories.

The thirty-year-old man may have a job, a wife, three kids, a house, care for himself, and two or three other responsibilities that God has given him: perhaps investment in an inner-city project, his role at church, or providing for an ailing mother-in-law. All of these form his field for this season in his life. He tends it all prayerfully, skillfully, with excellence, and to the glory of God in concert with a band of brothers. He, too, prospers. He, too, grows.

The Heart of Noble Manhood

Single or married, young or old, whatever race or profession—with each new season of life, with each new God-assigned field, there is a redefinition. New boundaries are drawn. New skills are needed. If we are faithful, there is an ever-broadening field. This is how a man grows. This is what God uses to prepare him for greater weight, greater authority, greater prosperity, and greater power to do ever more meaningful good in the world.

Tend your field. Do it to the glory of God. Do it realizing you cannot do it alone. You need God and a band of brothers. But do it passionately. All the features of righteous, noble manhood will emerge from your life as you do.

Manly men tend their field. It is not all a good and noble man needs to know. It is, though, the beginning. It is the heart.

Now you know. Now you can take your field in hand. Now you can see the need for a devoted band of brothers more clearly than ever.

Time to Build

1. Describe the "field" God has given you to tend in this current season of your life. What people, things, priorities, and tasks are part of this field? To the best of your ability, do you know your field, protect your field, and make sure that everything in your field flourishes according to the will of God? If not, what are some of the ways in which you have fallen short?

2. How could having a band of brothers help you tend your current field?

3. Stephen described two types of men who have been ignoring the field God gave them—the one who ignores his family's needs, and the other who neglects his field just as much but covers it up with money and other superficialities. Can you relate to either of these men? Are you like one of these men? Was your father like one of these? What happens to a man's field when it is ignored and neglected?

THE FIVE ESSENTIALS OF
A BAND OF BROTHERS

Now we get to it. We begin to drill down into the factors that distinguish a band of brothers. Since I want you to ponder these thoroughly, put them into practice, and teach them to others, I'm going to lay them before you in a numbered list. I do not claim that this is the list to end all lists when it comes to men and their band of brothers. Still, these are the features of the kind of band of brothers every man needs and all men must learn to build.

1. The Indirect Connection

Most bands of brothers, like most male friendships, begin with an indirect connection. This simply means that the men involved get to know each other by doing something "indirect," something other than digging into each other's lives or asking tough questions or trying to process deep and emotional things. They watch a game or they fix something or they throw some meat on the grill. In other words, they relate to each other first by doing something other than relating. This is how men connect to each other and it is nearly always the start of everything meaningful among them.

Women are different. They can go deep with each other nearly from the moment they meet. They have relational abilities most men don't have. Men, however, need something else to do together before they start relating directly.

There have been studies done in which little boys and girls are put in a room with chairs and toys. When the girls are put in the room and told they can move things around as they wish, they routinely position chairs facing each other. The little girls then sit in the chairs and look into each other's faces. After a while, one of them is likely to say something like, "I like your hair" or "That's a cute dress." The point is, they face each other immediately and engage. They don't need other activities in order to relate to each other. The relating is their activity.

Now, little boys will also move the chairs but they move them side by side. Then they sit shoulder to shoulder and look around the room together. Eventually, one of them will suggest something they can do. "I bet I can beat you arm wrestling," one will challenge. Or maybe it's, "Wanna play catch?" It might be,

"I bet we can stack those blocks to the ceiling" or "I wonder if we can make Tommy pull us in that wagon." Whatever it is, the boys look for something to do together. It's how they relate to each other: by *doing*.

This is simply the way of men. They love to be together but don't ask them to get all intense and relational the minute they walk in the door. The game has to be on and the steaks have to be cooking. Someone needs to pick up a guitar and get the groove started. The court needs to be free for some pick-up basketball and some cans of something good to drink need to be on ice. The house damaged in the storm has to be fixed and fifty men need to throw themselves into the work all while jokes and smack talk fill the air. This is how men get to know each other. They ramp up. They size each other up in the doing. They get comfortable while in motion.

He who would master the art of bringing men together must master the art of the indirect connection. Almost everything meaningful among men starts indirectly. It is the way of things. It's also a lot of fun.

2. The Extension of Honor

This indirect connection among men usually leads to friendship. Yet a group of friends isn't a band of brothers yet.

What usually takes friendships to the next level is when one man honors the exceptional gifts of another man and makes this honor part of the meaning of the friendship.

I've always loved the words that the seer Samuel wrote when he was describing how Jonathan, the son of King Saul, saw the greatness in David and honored him. Samuel wrote, "After David had finished talking with Saul, Jonathan became one in spirit with David, and he loved him as himself."[4]

David had just killed Goliath, showing exceptional courage and skill. Jonathan loved what he saw in David's life. His ferocity. His passion for Israel. His bravery. His martial skill. Jonathan had to have the friendship of this man. So, he "became one in spirit" with David. Jonathan honored David and made honor a feature of the friendship between the two men.

This is how it works. Two men are friends. One of them wants to take the friendship to a deeper, more fulfilling level. So, he turns to his friend and says, "You know, you are in great shape. I admire that. The discipline. The strength. I really respect you for it. Tell me, where did you get your devotion to working out and eating right?"

Now, this expression of honor takes some humility. Most men are too busy trying to impress each other for one of them to honor the other. Yet when one man honors another truthfully and genuinely, it says some important things. First, it says, "I see you. I can tell what kind of man you are. I respect you." Second, it says, "You've got gifts I don't have. I'm impressed. I like that we're different. What you are is meaningful to me." Finally, there is an assumed invitation: "Teach me. I want to draw from the good in your life. Let's make this friendship, in part, about helping each other be better."

The extension of honor makes a friendship that has largely been about shared enjoyments into a friendship that is also about shared purpose. This may be a subtle shift but once it happens it lays the foundation for all that comes afterward—two or more men spurring each other on to be better men.

That's the turn. That's the beginning. Honor becomes the basis for friendship, for fun, and for achieving together.

3. The Covenant Transition

Once two or more men turn their friendship toward helping each other ascend in some way, it opens a door for them to help each other in the deepest ways. Perhaps a group of friends just has fun at first. They eat. They cheer on their team together. They take a hunting trip, shoot hoops, or get together to play music one night a week. It's all fun. Then, because one of them honors another, to the fun is added some encouragement and maybe a little teaching. One guy helps the others drop weight or learn how to tune an engine or figure out how to invest their money more wisely.

When fun and help mix together among men, a covenant transition is possible. This happens when two or more men make helping each other in some critical area of their lives a part of the purpose of the relationship.

It can happen as simply as this:

Jim, I've noticed that you and your wife have a genuine romance. You really love each other, you keep the fires burning with touch and words and gifts and serving, and you are both so happy in your marriage. That isn't the way it is at our house. I grew up without a dad. My mother drank and ran around. I just never saw anything like what you two are building at your place. Can you help me? I mean, can you show me how to win my wife's heart?

Jim, of course, says yes. He'll help. The two shake hands. Maybe they pray. Maybe Jim recommends a book or two and says they'll talk more over a burger the next week. What has happened is that covenant transition. A friendship filled with fun and encouragement also has become about helping a man with one of his deepest needs.

Or maybe it's a handful of men looking to one guy in their group for some help. Maybe they're mired in porn or need to drop some weight or maybe they have sons they don't understand or perhaps need to learn to define their field better so they can tend it with diligence. So, the one guy helps his buddies. In six weeks, perhaps who is helping and who is receiving changes. Or maybe everyone is both helping and receiving at the same time. This is all fruit of a covenant transition. It all happens because men have agreed to stand with each other on the battle lines of their lives.

One of my closest friends says that "a band of brothers often starts with two men and a drafted mentor." It's true. This is because the covenant transition turns friends into allies in the battle for great manhood.

4. The Free Fire Zone

Now, gentlemen, this is the sweet spot. This is what we are shooting for. This is where it all comes together.

You may be familiar with the words "free fire zone," particularly if you've served in the military. It usually means the zone of a battlefield in which a soldier may fire freely, in which he may shoot as he deems necessary.

When it comes to building a band of brothers, a "free fire zone" is created by an agreement among everyone in the band that anything that must be said to make a man better will be said. Each man extends to his brothers the right to address what needs to be addressed—gently, respectfully, with intent to build and not hurt—to help make him the man God intended.

This condition is almost literally what separates the men from the boys. Many a man becomes a true man when he turns to his band of faithful men and says,

> *Listen, I intend to be the noble man I am called to be.*
> *I'm not there yet. Not by a long way. I know you dudes*
> *see what I can't see about myself. When you know I need*
> *to deal with something and I can't see it, you tell me. I*
> *insist. No hand-wringing. No wondering who's going to*
> *step up. You just tell me straight out what you see and*
> *then help me fix it. I'll do the same. That's the deal.*
> *Agree?*

Men thrive in this arrangement. It breeds confidence because each man trusts that his buddies have his back. It breeds moral courage because every man knows he has allies in his fight for noble manhood. It is a condition in which men grow; they grow together and they do it having the fun that men are made to have with each other.

My band of brothers loves me and I revere them, but they spare me nothing. They aren't afraid of me. They aren't going to put up with anything but my best. They guard me constantly. They never cease to say what needs to be said and it usually gets said on the racquetball court or over a pizza or after a movie. But it gets said and then it gets dealt with.

You need to keep in mind that our whole culture works against the concept of a band of brothers. It certainly works against the idea of a free fire zone. In the American South, we are all too polite to invade a man's space and in the North you aren't supposed to get too personal and out West we're all supposed to be too tough and rugged to be approachable.

Bull!

We're just men. We have our gifts but we also have our damage and we're blind to most of it. We need buddies—for fun, for rowdiness, and for inspiration—and we need courageous fellow warriors who will tell us what we need to know and stick close until we fix it. This is what men do.

Only fools live otherwise. Only cowards watch a friend destroy himself and never say a word.

Hear this. Every man you care about is fighting a great battle. Join him. Make him better. Help him win. Invite others into the great battles of your life. This is what a free fire zone is. Don't go through life without it!

> ## 5. The Contagious Culture <

Where these four features of a band of brothers exist—
the indirect connection, the extension of honor, the covenant
transition, and the free fire zone—a culture grows. This culture
is the environment in which manhood thrives, men get whole,
victories are won, and destined territory is claimed. It is this
culture that makes life in a band of brothers such a transforming experience.

We should define the word *culture* before we go further.
The word is often used of the arts. It evokes symphonies, ballet,
painting, and soaring architecture in our minds. This is a valid
use of the word and it is why we might say of someone that they
are "cultured." They are sophisticated and knowledgeable in the
arts, perhaps even in philosophy and history, for example.

Here, though, we are leaning to the other definition of
culture, which refers to "what is encouraged to grow." It is a
condition created by what is prized, what is valued, what is
emphasized, and what is celebrated. To put it a bit more techni-
cally, culture is the externalizing of what we believe. It is how we
live out our faith, our values, and our view of the world.

Let's stick to that first, easier definition: "culture is what
is encouraged to grow." In this sense, everyone creates a culture around them. You've experienced this. Perhaps you've
spent time with a friend and when you are done you are excited,

48

encouraged, feeling bold, eager for challenge, and hungry to improve yourself in some area. You feed upon what that man encourages to grow and it changes you.

You've also probably spent time with a friend or with a group of guys and when your time was done you felt like you needed a shower. They cut into each other with their words. They talked about nothing but nastiness. They used foul language, described disgusting things in great detail, and had no respect for God or man. You felt slimed. You felt small. You felt dirty. Their culture tainted you.

This would be a good moment for you to ponder what kind of culture you produce. What do you encourage to grow? What do you feed others from the garden of your life? Is it bitter and self-pitying? Is it angry and resentful? Is it fun and energizing? Is it noble and elevating? What kind of culture do you build? What do you encourage to grow in the lives around you?

It is an important question for you because, if you're going to be a valued part of a band of brothers as I describe them in these pages, you are going to have to take responsibility for building a culture. You're going to have to help create a way of relating among your group of men that is fun and energetic, honoring of each man, devoted to helping each man win his battles, and utterly given to doing whatever is necessary for each man to arise to his best. In other words, you must invest yourself completely in a culture of vision, honor, sacrifice, courage, morality, and labor—all wrapped in fun and manly joy along the way.

This is the goal of a band of brothers: an ennobling culture of righteous manhood. The indirect connect, the extension of honor, the covenant transition, and the free fire zone are what get us to this goal. These are how we arrive at a culture that makes a band of brothers work for the good of every man.

I want to urge you to start asking the "culture question" of your life, of your family's life, of your work, and of the men you know. Ask it constantly. Ask it courageously. Look the answers in the face. What do you encourage to grow in the lives around you? What do people take away from time with you? What is the culture of your home and your family? What is the culture you share with your friends?

Here is the truth: Culture rules. Culture wins. Culture shapes everything. The most important part of leadership, parenting, and friendship is culture building. It is how you determine what is encouraged to grow in the environments you are responsible for.

This is why all true bands of brothers arrive at a culture that makes every man in them better. This is what is contagious about a band of brothers. It is the thing every man takes away and reproduces in the lives of others. The culture. The way of being. The fruit of the things that are esteemed.

The Five Essentials of a Band of Brothers

If a man spends a few hours among his band of brothers, he ought to leave feeling esteemed, feeling stronger than before, and feeling the boldness that comes from accepting a mission as part of a group of men. He should have increased passion to be good, greater inner fire to win his fights, and a deeper hunger to do noble things in the lives of others. He should also be wiser, better informed, and more equipped to fulfill his purpose. Also, if he's not laughing at the fun he's had, feeling the effects of a good meal, and looking forward to the next trip or project everyone's discussing, well, then the noblest culture possible hasn't prevailed yet.

A band of brothers builds a culture. They get there through action, honor, covenant, and courageous transparency. Once that culture permeates every man's life in the band of brothers, change is coming to the world. There's about to be a whole lot of fun, a whole lot of rebuilding of men, and a whole lot of good poured into the lives each man touches. This is why a manly culture is at the heart of every true band of brothers.

Time to Build

1. Do you agree that there are five "essentials" to building a band of brothers? If not, what would you add to Stephen's list? Of these five essentials, which ones come most naturally to you? Which ones call for you to develop new skills and practices?

2. What benefits are there to a "free fire zone" among a band of brothers? What concerns or hesitations do you have about being involved in such an honest group of men? Why have previous groups of men you've been a part of not fully achieved this "free fire zone"?

3. Is the culture you produce with your life more positive—fun, energizing, noble, elevating, encouraging? Or is it more negative—angry, bitter, selfish, uncaring? In what ways do you need to change the culture you are creating in order to be part of a successful, encouraging, and honorable band of brothers?

TIME OUT!

I'M ABOUT TO GIVE YOU A LIST OF PRACTICAL STEPS FOR BUILDING YOUR band of brothers and then I'm heading to a close. Because I'm going to give you another list, it is essential that I tell you something right here and right now. It is also essential that you never forget it.

Here it is. There is no one model for a band of brothers. There is no one pattern. There are essentials. There are important features. Hear me, though: There is absolutely no single pattern.

Remember what I have said several times thus far. *A band of brothers is not a meeting, a club, a therapy group, or a self-help society. It is the group of men you do life with. It is the team of brothers who are committed to great manhood with you. It is the band of men you build a manly culture with, a culture of inspiration and improvement.*

This means that bands of brothers are as diverse as the men committed to them. I can describe a thousand different ways I've see bands of brothers done. One band I know processes the principles of noble manhood while they work out and sit in the sauna. Once in a while they digest a good book on manhood together or they watch a video series. When they do this, they schedule a "Steak Fest." Most of the discussing happens while everyone is chomping on a T-bone.

One weekend a month they go together to repair an inner-city school. They also have very specific manhood initiation ceremonies for their sons. Occasionally they spend time screaming at their teams on TV. They are all fiercely devoted to each other and as tough on each other as they can be. They won't be satisfied until each one of them achieves his highest in every manly pursuit.

I also know bands of military brothers who do all their confronting and processing on long runs. I'm talking about a couple of marathons a week. Once a year they go away to hunt or do an Ironman competition. They eat. They laugh. They read. They learn. What happens in the band of brothers stays in the band of brothers. If a guy in their band gets transferred to a new post, they stay connected by conferencing online. Wherever they are reassigned, they are expected to grow a new band of men. Their previous band of brothers holds them accountable for this.

Time Out!

I know New York accountants who meet online every week during a lunch hour. They do a lot of other things together, too, but the Tuesday Online Lunch is sacred.

I know London airline pilots who arrange their travel so they can all spend a day together at an airport hotel once a quarter. They also connect through emails, phone calls, online conferencing, or a restaurant meeting at an airport when a few of them manage to land in the same place for a while.

I know carpenters who do all their talking on the job and take a hunting trip together twice a year. This might all sound a bit chummy but these guys are harder on each other than any other band of brothers I know.

I know a band of brothers completely made up of players in the National Football League. They bark at each other while bench-pressing 350 pounds and call each other constantly while on the road to make sure all is clean and right in each other's lives. Once a year, they bunker in at someone's house, send the ladies away, and do an annual checkup on everything important. It works for them. That's all that matters. They are all thriving as righteous men.

All the successful groups I've seen have these characteristics: there is some means of constant contact, there is always some kind of regular get-together, there is almost always some material on manhood to digest, there is plenty of free-flowing chat time, and there is nearly always a trip or a project scheduled once or twice a year. Food and laughter are ever-present.

These are about the only common traits of the bands I know other than the ones I listed in the previous chapter. Beyond this, every variation in the world prevails. The central issue is not structure. The central issue is going deep and coaching each other to maximum manhood. Everything else is optional.

Hear me: There are endless variations. There is no pattern. There are only the essentials lived out as personalities, national and ethnic cultures, and time constraints dictate or allow. I love them all.

I do have to say that my favorite guys are the London pilots. They told me that they often process with each other while they fly, which means that what they say to each other gets captured on their flight voice recorders. They joke that they can never have an accident because the investigators will hear all of their personal details. Of course, they're just kidding, but I do like the idea of a cockpit full of men talking about their lives during a moonlit flight to the other side of the world.

Time to Build

1. Which of the common characteristics of successful groups that Stephen describes have been missing from your previous or current men's group? Why do you think they were not a facet of the group? How might including some of the characteristics Stephen lists have changed you and the other men you met with?

2. Stephen wrote, "The central issue is going deep and coaching each other to maximum manhood. Everything else is optional." What keeps most men's groups from "going deep"? What do you think is involved in coaching another man to maximum manhood? Can you think of a time when your dad, coach, or another mentor coached you to maximum manhood?

3. What concerns you most about being in a band of brothers that dares to go deep with you and challenge you? What excites you about being in such a brotherhood?

FIVE TRUTHS FOR BUILDING YOUR BAND OF BROTHERS

THOUGH THERE IS NO DEFINITIVE PATTERN FOR BANDS OF BROTHERS, there are some practical matters I want to make sure you know. These will save you time, spare you a mess, and move you more steadily to the heart of what a band of brothers can mean.

1. The Indirect Connection—Again!

Let me start by returning to the all-important matter of the indirect connection. If you want to lead or influence men— or if you just want to have a lot of good friends—you have to master the art of the indirect connection. It's not difficult but it is something you have to be intentional about.

Men are action-oriented. Men want to be up and doing. Ask a man what his favorite times with other men have been in his life and he is likely to describe experiences when he and his buddies were building something or going somewhere. There was action. There was teaming. There was a goal. These are important to men.

There is more to this than just fun. It is while doing something that men size each other up. Men are scanners. They survey the scene. They identify character and notice traits. Most men do this quickly. The guy who constantly stops and talks while other men are working is noticed. The guy who won't stop playing around is noticed too. The dude who makes a big show of his knowledge but can't ever get the job right is noted. This is how men evaluate each other.

Remember the story about Jonathan and David I mentioned earlier? Notice that Jonathan wasn't drawn to David's words. He was drawn to the way David conducted himself on the battlefield. David's actions told Jonathan what he needed to know. David's actions revealed his spirit and Jonathan took note. This is the way it is with most men.

So the indirect connection provides opportunity for men to bond because it allows them to see each other in action. If you want to construct a band of brothers, you'll have to create ways for men to do things together. The game. The barbecue. The run. The bluegrass pickin' party. The day of fishing. The hunt. The drum circle. The work to be done on the elderly couple's house. The day with the neighborhood boys. Anything. Everything. Whatever righteous things men love to do with other men.

Keep in mind that this need for the indirect connection among men never ends. Even when men know each other fully and have walked together for years, they still don't want to walk in a room, circle up some chairs, and have to talk about their deepest feelings and thoughts right away. Give a man some space! Give him some time! Give him a chance to feel the situation. Give him a laugh and a brisket sandwich, for heaven's sake, before we ask him to talk about anything meaningful. Men won't stay involved if everything is internal and emotional all the time. Give a man something to do with other men. All else comes from this.

Above all, don't ever, ever forget this eternal truth. The most important words for impacting men are these: "Let's eat!"

2. The Art of 3B

When you start looking for men to build a band of brothers with, your high-yield candidates are going to be the friends you already have. Even if these are just guys you shoot hoops with or joke around with after work, they will still be your wisest starting point. Your challenge with these relationships is turning them from being friendships only to being brothers in the cause of great manhood also. We call this "3B-ing them."

My band of brothers came up with this shorthand by taking the words "building a band of brothers" and shortening it to "3B." So when one of my guys is teaching another man how to move a friendship toward something deeper, he'll say, "Well, you'll have to 3B him." It means our guy will have to turn the friendship toward band of brothers themes.

To 3B a man is simply to start a conversation that nudges a sports friendship or a work friendship or a workout friendship toward the battle for great manhood. It can be as simple as this: "Dude, we've been hanging out at the gym for a long time. There are some real babes down here. Man, tell me, how do you keep it clean? I mean, do you have to battle the porn, the fantasy, and the burn for the ladies that I do? Help me. Or at least tell me you're in the same battle."

A step toward openness like this helps you and your friend locate each other on the Manly GPS. It opens a door to teaming up in one of the great battles for righteous manhood. Your friend might tell you he's not fighting against anything and that in fact it's his goal to get with every lady he can. Well, that answer might be disappointing to you but at least you'll have located your buddy on the Manly GPS. If he says that he has to fight the burn for the ladies all the time and then asks how you manage it, something important has begun. Two men are talking about how to be better men. They are admitting a struggle for noble manhood. They're asking each other for help. That friendship has just received a dose of 3B. Great things are possible from this moment on.

So you start your hunt for a band of brothers by 3B-ing your existing friendships. Over time, you'll gain more friendships. You'll want to 3B those too. All this means is that you gently open up a chance to deal with something meaningful in the battle for noble manhood. I've been sitting nearby when this has happened with other men. Some of the great topics they opened up with were:

- What's the best book on being a good man that you've ever read?

- What's the hardest thing about being a man for you?

- Who in your life taught you the most about being a good man?

- What do you think is going on with the pitiful state of manhood these days? What are the answers?

- What's the one experience that has most shaped you as a man?

- Man, I really battle lust/drinking/bitterness/violence. Got any answers for me?

· Dude, what the heck is going on with our sons?

· When I watched that movie, I saw the kind of man I want to be like. Did you feel the same way?

You see how it goes. You simply open up a bit and let a friend step into great manhood with you. Or maybe you do the stepping. It doesn't matter exactly how it goes. What matters is that a friendship that has largely been about basketball and beer or music and sushi becomes about two men stepping into each other's fight for true manhood.

It starts with a talk.

It moves to a goal.

It thrives on encouragement.

It strengthens through knowledge.

It achieves through partnership.

This is how you 3B your friendships and enlist your buddies in the grand fight for manhood in our generation.

3. The Brotherhood of the Fierce

Most of the bands of brothers I know have a lot of fun and would be worth the time just for that. Yet I have never known of a band that truly grows righteous manhood in which there is not a fierce devotion to each other's good. By fierce I mean courageous, unsparing, tough as it needs to be, hard-hitting, and completely invested.

They don't wound each other unnecessarily. They don't treat each other's feelings casually. They care deeply for each other. Yet they will wound a man if that is what his masculine growth requires. This is what I mean by the Brotherhood of the Fierce.

Building this dynamic into your band of brothers will require the following:

Be Bold

For a band of brothers to work as it should, the men involved must not be afraid to go after anything that hinders great manhood. The challenge to this will be different for every man. Some men will have to be coaxed into telling the truth. Other men will have to dare to ask the tough questions. All men will have to invest themselves in fixing what's broken in each other's lives.

Building Your Band of Brothers

Time and again in my band of brothers, I've had to say things like this:

- *Listen, nothing will shock me. Out with it!*

- *How are you doing? And I'm not just saying hello. What's up with you?*

- *If you don't get honest, you're not going to get right. Cut to the chase already.*

- *Cut the crap! I love you. You know that. Tell me what's really going on.*

Other men have had to say things like this to me as well. We are all human. We all want people to think well of us. We all tend to hide ugly realities about ourselves. A band of brothers is the group of men who love you but aren't afraid of you. They'll run you over to get at the truth and then help you heal up from the very wounds they inflicted!

Keep this in mind. The price of growth in a band of brothers is unswerving boldness. Hunt down what's wrong and fix it. This is how it works in the free fire zone we've all agreed to.

Challenge

Every man needs to be challenged by other men. Make this part of your culture as well. If a man mentions to you that he's a hundred pounds heavier than he was in high school, you can't just let that go. You say, "Listen, we're going to start walking together. Get serious about this. I want to see you forty pounds lighter by June. C'mon, you can do this. We'll do it together."

You'll have to find your own way of expressing these things, but work to get good at it and make it part of your manner with the men you're committed to. Challenge them with specific goals for the critical battles of their lives. Then be with them in the execution of the solution.

Let me say a hard thing. We've all got friends whose language is atrocious or who eat so sloppily at a table they make you want to throw up or who speak too harshly to their wives or who dress like bums. They will never change unless someone cares enough to point out what needs to change and offers help. If cowardice rules, change won't happen. If loving boldness rules, men thrive.

Please don't hear me saying that being in a band of brothers is license to go off on a man about everything wrong in his life all at once. It isn't. A band of brothers isn't a branch of the local Snot-Nosed Critics Society. It is, though, a group of courageous friends who will speak to each other about anything that hinders great manhood.

So, challenge each other. Do it kindly. Do it firmly. Be part of the solution. We'll all grow together. We'll respect each other for the tough love that made us better.

Assign

We don't want to control the men around us or turn them into our students. We do want to spur them on to the greatness intended for them. This sometimes means pushing them to do things they need to do and making them accountable for results.

It sounds something like this: "Listen, you admit to neglecting your wife. Here's the deal. That woman will receive a gift, a night out, and time with you the way she wants it. There will also be five sincere, creative compliments and lots of touch every day. You've got two weeks, big boy. I want to hear back from you. I don't want to hear romantic details. I want to hear about a woman whose life is changing for the better. Get on it."

That's how it goes. Does this scare you? Then take a moment to put the assignment above into your own words. Practice. Get ready. Men don't get better unless they have a goal and someone fighting alongside them who holds them accountable. The men in your band of brothers need for you to get good at this. Find your game. Hone it. Use it. Destinies are in the balance.

Encourage

Some of us came from warm and supportive homes. Some of us came from homes where an encouraging word was never heard. Whatever your background, we're here now. We're committed now. Know this: A band of brothers runs on encouragement.

For a man to change, he needs to hear that his band of brothers believes in him, that they know he will overcome. Encouragement of this kind has to be expressed and demonstrated constantly to all the men near you, to all who feed on the contagious culture of manhood around you.

This means you'll have to be ready to urge your men along with sincere encouragement like this: "Look, you are better than this. I've seen you overcome huge obstacles. Get busy on this one." Or, "Buddy, you put your mind to this, you're going to kick this thing to the curb. Your kids will be telling their grandkids about this victory."

Plan it. Mean it. Demonstrate it. Lives will change because you do.

Before I leave this topic of the Brotherhood of the Fierce, I want to tell you a story. A band of brothers I know has some fine men in it. Two are former NFL players. One is a wealthy entrepreneur.

One is an accountant. Another is the manager of a café. They are wonderful men. They've helped each other grow and had a blast together over a lot of years.

Not too long ago, one of these dudes had an affair. When it came to light, he left town and hid in a house he owned in Colorado. Well, his band of brothers wasn't having it. When they found out, they were furious. He'd been lying to them. So they all flew to Colorado and drove to this dude's house.

When they pulled up, they realized they didn't have a key. No problem. The former NFL defensive tackle among them kicked in the door. Yes. That's what I said. He kicked in the door of a million-dollar home. The other guys quickly got ahead of him so he didn't murder the trembling fool hiding upstairs.

Thankfully, everyone cooled down. Listen, though. These dudes kept that guy in his house for a week. They made him tell his story, made him hear their disappointment, made him pray with them, and made him commit to going home and making it work. With all this done, they fixed the front door and went home.

The man's wife took him back. From the start, she said she was willing to try to make the marriage work because she trusted the band of brothers even if she didn't quite trust her husband at the time. The marriage healed. The kids opened their hearts to their dad again. All is well now.

That band of brothers was a fierce brotherhood. They literally threatened to pound that man if he did not start making sense. They stood by the family, took the kids out to lunch, and let them talk as much as they needed to and hammered that idiot husband until he got right. A family was healed. A legacy restored. When it was all done, that three-hundred-pound defensive tackle said these sweet words: "You ever even think about doing something that stupid again and I'll kill you." I don't know if he was kidding.

Fierce. Brotherhood.

Live it.

4. Get in the Home

For a band of brothers to do its job, it has to appear in each man's home occasionally. This just means that the men play pickup basketball in the driveway and then have some lunch. It means there's some grilling happening on the patio before the game. It means each guy hosts a food fest at his place. Anything that puts his brothers in his home once in a while.

We don't want to invade privacy. We don't want to know details of the bank account or the bedroom unless helping the man requires it and he agrees. We do want to be a presence in the family of every man. We do want to know his wife, put an arm around his kids, and see how he lives.

My wife knows who the men around me are. She has their phone numbers. They check on her from time to time. I've told her that if she ever thinks I'm flipping out, call them. Don't hesitate. If I'm out of town and she needs something, call them. If our children are in trouble and I'm on the other side of the world, call them. You can't believe the look of peace that settles on her face when I say these things.

A band of brothers needs to be in each other's lives as fully as needed, as fully as allowed. This means we've got to know how our men are living and how they treat their families. It means we want the wife and children of every man to know they have backup if they ever need it. They are safe. Think of what these words must mean to a family, particularly in our troubled modern world: "We are standing with your husband and your dad. We've got him and, because we do, we've also got you. Let's do this together."

5. Bring in the Boys

There is an African proverb that goes like this: "If we do not initiate the boys, they will burn the village down." This is what's happening in our world today. From street gangs to radical Islam, from skinheads to high school kids who shoot up their proms, un-fathered, un-mentored, un-initiated young men are troubling the world.

One of the tasks of every band of brothers is to initiate the boys.

This can be as casual as the fathers in your band of brothers involving their sons from time to time when they come of age or it can be a serious initiation ceremony when a boy reaches adolescence. Bands of brothers the world over do this differently, according to their culture and their customs.

In most every case, something takes place much like the bar mitzvah of our Jewish friends. When a Jewish boy enters adolescence and proves himself, he is made a "son of the covenant." He commits himself more deeply to God. He embraces his responsibilities among his people. He's viewed differently by his mother and sisters. He owns his role in the community and thus the community owns him in the most respectful and liberating way. In short, he becomes a man. More importantly, he becomes a man among men.

I've seen it done a thousand ways. Some men put together an event in which their sons' friends, coaches, and teachers give testimonies and issue challenges. There is usually a gift symbolizing this milestone—a sword, a plaque, or some other object that will last a lifetime. Always, there is food.

Other men I know create a training program that culminates in a ceremony like I've described. Before the boy is welcomed into manhood, he has to perform community services, hike a great distance, memorize a large portion of manly text, maybe master a song on his guitar, or improve his bench press. Sometimes he has to heal a relationship. In one case, the young man was required to get the approval of ten men before he was finally accepted. Trust me, it changed his life.

Keep in mind that this initiation is not just for biological sons either. It is for the young men in the neighborhood. It is for the boys you know who have no men in the home. It is for sons of the heart, sons of the tribe. It is righteous men putting their arms around future men and sealing manhood into their souls.

Whatever the method of initiation and however formally or informally it is done, a band of brothers brings sons into the contagious culture of manhood. This is how the older generation sets the younger generation on its way in the world. They challenge them. They guard them. They honor them. They call them out as men. They celebrate them.

I cannot overemphasize how much manhood in our time demands this. Do it. Do it broadly. Do it deeply. A generation of men is waiting.

Time to Build

1. Stephen emphasizes the importance of the "indirect connection." Why do you think such connections are necessary? Have you been a part of men's groups that overlooked the importance of this type of connection? Why would this strategy not succeed with most men?

2. How would you feel if one of your more casual friends started "3B-ing you"? Why do we often prefer the more casual friendship than the kind it takes to be a part of a band of brothers?

3. What are some of the excuses we use for not attempting to be bold with a fellow man and challenge him to greater manhood? Is remaining silent an acceptable course of action when you notice a friend struggling? Why or why not? Who in your life would you like to join you in a "brotherhood of the fierce"? When will you talk with him about this?

A BAND OF BROTHERS CHECKLIST

Now, gentlemen, let's put it all together. Because this book is a hard-hitting call to action, it is fitting that we should end it with a guide for taking that action. As we've seen, there is no single pattern for a band of brothers, but there are some wise steps you should know for building your band of brothers. The following checklist will guide you through some of those steps and help you live out all that we've seen in this book.

By the way, don't ponder these steps alone. Use them as a basis for discussion with the people whose counsel you trust. Remember that in all things we are better together than we are alone. These steps are no different.

1. Reflect on the people, experiences, and thinking that have brought you to your current state of manhood. What do you find that is good and noble? What needs repair?

2. Assess the friendships you've had throughout your life. Look for patterns and tendencies in your approach to friendship. What do you find that will help you build a band of brothers? What do you find that you need to change?

3. Take stock of the men in your life and identify which ones might be good partners in helping to build a band of brothers. Ask God to guide you.

4. Consider giving some of the men you know copies of this book, or perhaps *Mansfield's Book of Manly Men,* or any other book about manhood that has been meaningful to you. When you do, notice which of your friends are inspired by what they read. These men will be good candidates for a band of brothers.

5. Start drawing your friends into conversations about noble manhood. Move toward the expressions of honor described in this book: *"Bob, you're good at relating to your kids. Can you help me with that?"*

6. Put together some opportunities for the men you know to connect indirectly. Pray for these get-togethers. Notice what boils to the surface from the lives of these men.

7. Once some men have joined you in meaningful chats about manhood, consider heading toward the all-important covenant transition. Keep making opportunities for indirect connections while you make this covenant transition with those men who are willing.

8. When the time is right, establish the vital "free fire zone." When this is in place, congratulations—you have the beginning of a band of brothers!

9. Try to assure the basics of the most successful bands of brothers: means of constant contact, regular get-togethers, books or audio/visual materials that feed noble manhood, plenty of free-flowing chat time, some kind of annual or semiannual getaway or adventure, huge amounts of food and laughter. Always encourage a "brotherhood of the fierce."

10. Never forget these words: "*A band of brothers is not a meeting, a club, a therapy group, or a self-help society. It is the group of men you do life with. It is the team of brothers who are committed to great manhood with you. It is the band of men you build a manly culture with, a culture of inspiration and improvement.*"

"We few,
We happy few,
We Band of Brothers."

NOTES

1. In 2016, the suicide rate for males of all ages and ethnicities was 21.31 per 100,000 population. For females it was 6.04. (Centers for Disease Control and Prevention, National Center for Injury Prevention and Control, Web-based Injury Statistics Query and Reporting System (WISQARS) [online], (2005) 2018 Mar 22. Available from URL: www.cdc.gov/injury/wisqars.)

2. This is one of the four "Manly Maxims" in *Mansfield's Book of Manly Men*.

3. 2 Corinthians 10:13, NIV.

4. 1 Samuel 18:1, NLT.

EIGHT BOOKS TO READ NEXT

On Noble Manhood
- *Wild at Heart: Discovering the Secret of a Man's Soul* by John Eldredge
- *Mansfield's Book of Manly Men: An Utterly Invigorating Guide to Being Your Most Masculine Self* by Stephen Mansfield

On The Psychology of Male Friendships
- *The Buddy System: Understanding Male Friendships* by Geoffrey L. Greif
- *Breaking the Male Code: Unlocking the Power of Friendship* by Robert Garfield

On Male Friendships and Community in History
- *Comrades: Brothers, Fathers, Heroes, Sons, Pals* by Stephen Ambrose
- *Tribe: On Homecoming and Belonging* by Sebastian Younger

On Boys
- *The Wonder of Boys: What Parents, Mentors and Educators Can Do to Shape Boys into Exceptional Men* by Michael Gurian
- *Raising a Modern Day Knight: A Father's Role in Guiding His Son to Authentic Manhood* by Robert Lewis

ABOUT THE AUTHOR

Stephen Mansfield is a New York Times bestselling author whose works include *The Faith of George W. Bush*, *The Search for God and Guinness*, *The Character and Greatness of Winston Churchill*, *Lincoln's Battle with God*, and *Mansfield's Book of Manly Men*. He is a popular speaker who also leads a media training firm based in Washington, DC. Mansfield lives in Nashville and his nation's capital with his wife, Beverly. To learn more, visit StephenMansfield.TV.

Join the GreatMan Movement

GREATMAN.TV

 @GreatManTV

 GreatMan.TV

 GreatMan.TV

For more about Stephen, visit

STEPHENMANSFIELD.TV